T0354737

When God Serves Restraining Orders

BARRED FROM GOING BACK TO CHURCH

RONALD F. SMITH

Order this book online at www.trafford.com
or email orders@trafford.com

Most Trafford titles are also available at major online book retailers.

© Copyright 2024 Ronald F. Smith.
All rights reserved. No part of this publication may be reproduced, stored in a retrieval
system, or transmitted, in any form or by any means, electronic, mechanical, photocopying,
recording, or otherwise, without the written prior permission of the author.

Print information available on the last page.

ISBN: 978-1-6987-1722-7 (sc)
ISBN: 978-1-6987-1723-4 (hc)
ISBN: 978-1-6987-1724-1 (e)

Library of Congress Control Number: 2024914481

Because of the dynamic nature of the Internet, any web addresses or links contained in
this book may have changed since publication and may no longer be valid. The views
expressed in this work are solely those of the author and do not necessarily reflect the
views of the publisher, and the publisher hereby disclaims any responsibility for them.

Any people depicted in stock imagery provided by Getty Images are models, and such images are
being used for illustrative purposes only.
Certain stock imagery © Getty Images.

Trafford rev. 08/28/2024

 www.trafford.com
North America & international
toll-free: 844-688-6899 (USA & Canada)
fax: 812 355 4082

Dedicated to my wife, Deirdere, and son, Joshua.

Dedicated to my wife, daughter and son.

My Wife Deirdere

As I sit down to pen these words, my heart is full of gratitude and my mind is awash with memories of the journey I embarked upon while writing this first book. This journey, filled with its highs and lows, was not one I walked alone. Besides me, every step of the way, was my incredible wife, whose unwavering support became the cornerstone of my resolve and the beacon that guided me through moments of doubt and despair. The early stages of writing a book are often filled with excitement and a fair dose of dreary. I was no exception. However, as the initial exhilaration waned and the daunting reality of the task ahead set in, it was your belief in me that stood as a bulwark against the tide of uncertainty. You were there to celebrate the completion of each chapter, to listen to my constant ramblings, and to offer your insights, which often shed light on solutions to narrative perplexes I struggled with. There were nights filled with frustration, days when words seemed to elude me, and moments when the end seemed nowhere in sight. During those times, your presence was a constant reminder of the reason I embarked on this journey. Your belief in my ability was exceptional, your encouragement unceasing. It was your confidence in me that often reignited my passion, your optimism that dispelled my pessimism. This book is but a small token of my love and gratitude for you. May it be a testament to the love that surrounds us, the challenges we've overcome together, and the endless adventures that await us. I am blessed to have you in my life and dedicate this achievement to you, my dear and darling wife. Let's celebrate many more milestones together.,

You Are the Winds Beneath My Wings,

Ron "The One",

My Son Joshua

From the inception of this book, you were my promoter. Your genuine interest in my work, your questions about things I experienced and your eagerness to know my weekly progress brought a sense of excitement and purpose that was profoundly motivating. Your belief in the value of my writing, even when I struggled to see it myself, was a gift that kept me grounded. Your encouragement came in various forms-sometimes it was the simple act of respecting my need for quiet and space to write, while at other times, it was your ridiculous humor, joyful anticipation for the new journey this book will take me that spurred me on. These acts, though seemingly small, were monumental in keeping my dream alive. In watching you, I relearned the importance of willpower. Just as you tackle your own challenges with determination and a positive spirit, you inspired me to approach my writing with the same attitude. Your resilience in the face of obstacles, your willingness to try again after a setback and change in direction, showed me the value of persistence. As I look back on this chapter of our lives, I am filled with pride-not just in the book I have written, but in the remarkable young man you are becoming in Christ.

Thank you for being my drum major and conductor.

Incomparable Fatherly Love,

Dad,

Gratitude

My Beloved Family and Cherished Berachah Congregation

As I reflect on the tumultuous times we've experienced together, words seem inadequate to express the depth of my gratitude for your unfailing support and encouragement. The journey we've embarked on, especially during the challenging period of our church split, has been profound growth, learning, and, ultimately, healing. It is through your steadfast love, prayers, and companionship that we have navigated these turbulent waters, emerging stronger and more united in our faith and purpose.

To my Family Members:
Sisters: Belinda & Patricia,
Nieces: Julillian & Brittany,
Nephew: Patrick
Great Nephew:
Aunt: Evelyn
First Cousin: Corey

As I stand today, reflecting on our journey through controversies, challenges, and milestones, I am filled with nothing but gratitude for having such a supportive family. In the midst of our lives, we encounter periods that test our resolve, challenge our faith, and ultimately, shape our destinies. These moments, while daunting, are made bearable through the support of those who stand by us-not out of obligation, but out of unconditional love and unwavering belief in our shared values and goals. It is to my beloved sisters, nieces, and nephew, the architects of my strength and the unsung heroes during our past trials, to whom I dedicate this book,

To my Church Members:

Your grace and patience during our times of division and uncertainty have been nothing short of inspirational. The way you rallied together, upholding our values of love, forgiveness, and unity, even when faced with discord, is a testimony to the true essence of our faith. Your encouragement for me to share our story through writing this book has been a source of immerse motivation. It is a privilege to journey alongside such compassionate and faithful individuals who embody Christ's teachings in every action. Your collective belief in the importance of sharing our story has been a powerful encouragement. This book, chronicling our journey through division towards reconciliation and growth, aims not only to narrate our experiences but to offer hope and guidance to others facing similar trials. Your stories, insights, and reflections have been invaluable in shaping this narrative, making it a mosaic of our shared trials and triumphs. Our journey has taught us the importance of collaboration, the power of forgiveness, and the unbreakable strength of a united church family. I am deeply grateful for each one of you. This book is a tribute to you all, a celebration of our collective spirit and faith in the face of adversity.

Appreciation

My Armorbearer Marvin

Marvin, As I reflect on the incredible voyage of writing my first book.

A journey, I must say, that would have been significantly more challenging without your unwavering support and relentless encouragement. From the very beginning, you believed in the potential of my story, even at times when I stop writing. Your faith in my abilities drove me pass writer's block. You were not just an assistant; you were my confidant, my sounding board, and, most importantly, my leaning post. I want you to know that your contributions have been invaluable not just to the book but to my personal growth as a writer, person and pastor. You have reminded me the importance of having caring people by your side who love, support and believe in you. As this book takes its final shape and prepares to meet its readers, I realize that it is not just my story that's being told but also a testament to our shared efforts, your incredible support, and determination in making this book become a reality.

Please accept my heartfelt gratitude for everything you have done. I look forward to embarking on many more projects with you by my side, confident in the knowledge that with your support, there is nothing we can't do.

Thank you, Marvin Jennings, for everything,

Warmest regards

Pastor Ronald Smith

To my Confidant Ullic Young

As I reflect on the last two and a half decades of our friendship, I am truly in awe of how much you have enriched my life. You have been more than a friend, comrade, and brother to me; but more like a soulmate, a steady source of wisdom, strength, and support.

Out of all the people in the world, God brought us together, as He did many characters in the Bible for a miraculous assignment and divine purpose. Our friendship has been a testament to God's perfect plan, filled with moments that have shaped and strengthened both of us.

You are one person who has been a constant in my life, no matter life circumstances. Your generosity of spirit, unwavering support, and faithfulness have left a lasting impact on me. I pray that, in some small way, I have also contributed to your life and that my presence has been as meaningful to you as yours has been to me.

As BFC was being birthed you were the midwife that held our hands, lead us through the pain and brought it to fruition. God knew that we needed someone with your expertise, dedication and a pure heart like Solomon to build His temple-and that, Ullic, is exactly what you did. Your commitment to nurturing and guiding the church has been instrumental in its growth and success.

Ullic, I am profoundly thankful for your friendship and the impact you have had on my life. Your presence and encouragement to write this book has been a blessing, and I look forward to many more years of shared experiences and growth.

With deepest appreciation and love,

Rev. Ron

Special Thanks

My Mentor Bruce Pittman

As I find myself reflecting on the journey we've embarked upon together - a journey that has culminated in the realization of a dream I've nurtured for many years: the completion of my first book. These words serve as a small token of my immense gratitude for the role you've played in this significant chapter of my life. When I first set out to write this book, I was acutely aware of the challenges that lay ahead. The task of translating my thoughts, experiences, and insights into a coherent and engaging narrative seemed daunting, if not insurmountable. However, your expertise, patience, and unwavering support transformed this daunting task into a journey of discovery and growth. From our initial discussions to the countless drafts and revisions, you have been more than just a composer; you have been a mentor, a confidant, and an invaluable collaborator. Your ability to listen deeply, to understand the essence of what I aimed to convey, and to articulate those ideas with clarity and eloquence has been nothing short of remarkable. Your dedication to this project was evident in every piece of advice you offered, and every effort you made to ensure that the final manuscript not only met but exceeded my expectations. Your meticulous attention to detail have brought my vision to life in ways I could never have imagined. I am immensely proud of what we have achieved together and am excited about the possibility of future collaborations.

With deepest gratitude,

Contents

1

CHAPTER

My Beginning

On October 29, 1961, I was born the youngest of Lesley and Helen Smith's four children. My oldest brother, Lesley, Jr., was seven years older than me. My sisters were named Belinda and Patricia.

Our childhood days on the south side of Albany, Georgia, were filled with uncertainty, unrest, and inadequacy in our home. My family was endlessly moving to find a larger and more affordable place, never staying in one house for more than a few years. However, I was hardly aware of the financial stress. My parents constantly clashed because my father was a tyrant. We were careful not to disrespect or upset him. My father had some spirits in him that were out to antagonize anyone who didn't submit to them. It was very peaceful and pleasurable whenever he wasn't around.

I distinctly remember one evening when I was playing in my bedroom with my toys when I thought I heard my father call my name. However, I was in no hurry to respond. When I entered his room, he shouted at me, "Didn't you hear me calling for you?"

"No sir. I didn't," I replied softly. Apparently, I didn't hear him the first time he called me, so he had hollered louder until I did.

3

He said, "I called you to turn the light off. The next time I call, you better stop whatever you are doing and come running."

Then he grabbed his pistol from the nightstand, aimed it toward the ceiling, and shot out the light bulb. I jumped at the sound of the gun, then turned around and closed the door, running back to my room, thankful he didn't shoot me. That was one of many traumatic encounters I had with my father growing up.

Outside of home, my life was enjoyable. We live in a good neighborhood. In the sixties, drugs and gangs were not a problem on the streets. We still had fights, as most kids do, but after we settled our arguments, we just went on like always and remained friends. Everyone was in the same boat, just trying to survive from one day to the next. We were always out roaming the streets from the time we woke up until we went to bed.

Early on, I had a heart for playing music, and I wanted to be in the band in middle school. However, I knew my parents couldn't afford to buy my favorite instrument, the trumpet. That was heart-breaking and embarrassing. I had to withdraw from music class, but I was too ashamed to tell the band director why. Thinking back, I believe it was a disappointment for my mother as well. She was a Sunday school pianist while pregnant with me, which contributed to my love for music. Even to this day, music is part of my heavenly gift. I still hope to pursue my dream and becoming proficient in playing an instrument.

When I was twelve years old, my parents decided to divorce. That changed everything for us. My father's departure from the household brought much relief from the abuse we had all been enduring. However, he refused to alimony and pay child support, which caused us to suffer financially. My mother was unable to work due to health problems, so we moved into housing projects and depended on the government and my grandparents for support.

Even though he didn't provide child support, I knew I could get some money from him when he got paid. I recall many times going inside a nightclub to get my snack money.

Several years later, my mother met and married a wonderful man who loved us dearly and showed the qualities of a real father, such as love, compassion, and generosity. His name was Richard Bennett. He was a hard-working man who took great care of us, so we no longer had to depend on outside sources for our basic needs. We were in desperate need of better furniture, so Mr. Richard purchased several bedroom sets, a large floor-model stereo, and the most beautiful piece of furniture we had ever owned—a red and white suede living room set. My mother took great pride in furnishing her home with it. She was also protective of it, covering the living room furniture with clear plastic to prevent it from getting dirty. No one was allowed to sit on it unless they were entertaining guests.

2

CHAPTER

Blinded By A Light

My first memorable Christmas present was a bicycle, courtesy of my stepfather. I was ecstatic when I woke up and saw it in the house. I still remember running, hugging and kissing him. That bicycle brought me so much joy because it was something I had always wanted for a very long time, and I was grateful to see it in the house that morning.

I remember exactly what it looked like—a sporty, yellow dirt bike with big tires, chopper handlebars, and a spring-loaded seat. I looked after my bike and kept it looking clean and shiny. I spent most of my days riding with my friends around the neighborhood. We were also on the hunt for money-making work like raking yards, picking up glass bottles to sell, running errands, or whatever we could do to make a little money. However, some of my friends weren't always a good influence on me. They regularly tempted me to do wrong, even calling me a coward when I refused. One day, I finally gave in to their pressure.

The one thing my bike did not have was a light so I could ride with my friends at night, so I saved up my money to purchase one. One morning my buddies and I rode to Gibson's Discount Store just to look around. After searching the sporting good department, I found the light I wanted to buy. However, I was disappointed because it cost more money than I had. I stood there holding the light in my hand, trying to figure out a way to get it. After a little while, I came up with a plan. I decided to take a lower price sticker from a less expensive item and placed it on the light. In my childish mind, this wasn't stealing because I would have enough money to pay for it then.

After switching the prices, I made my way to the cash register. My heart was pounding because I was a moment away from having my light. The cashier picked up the light and ranged it up. When I started to hand her the money a man in line behind me grabbed my arm and told the cashier to void the transaction and give him the light. I was scared and told him to let me go. He said, "No, you're going to jail." I began hollering for my friends to help me, but they were nowhere around. He started pulling me away from the register and I started crying and calling out for my momma, even though I knew she wasn't there.

He pulled me to an office in the back of the store and told me I was under arrest for shoplifting. I started pleading my case, but to no avail. I promised him that if he let me go, I would never steal again. He told me to stop crying and to give him my name, age, parents' names, and other information. I did, and once I calmed down, I started planning my escape. I told him I needed to go to the restroom, and he told me to go in my pants or wait until I got to the police station.

Within just a few moments, someone knocked on the office door. "This is my lucky break," I thought to myself, believing

I could run out the door when he opened it. When he did, my heart sank—a police officer was standing there. The security guard told him he wanted me arrested for shoplifting. Then the police officer put handcuffs on me and told him he would handle it. We started walking to the front of the store to his car. I was so embarrassed and kept my head down and eyes closed all the way. I could feel people staring at me. When we got outside, I looked up and saw my buddies sitting on their bikes, eating snacks. I guess they were waiting on me to come out but not like this. They looked dumbfounded and started pointing and whispering. I thought to myself, "They steal all the time and never get caught. Why me?"

The officer put me in the back seat and loaded my bike in the trunk. I was terrified and started bawling because I didn't know when I would see my family or friends again. I began trying to figure out a way to escape from his car. To my surprise, there were no inside doorknobs or window handles. The closer we got to the police station, the more frantic I became. When we arrived, the officer escorted me down a very long corridor and into a room where a man was seated at a desk. He introduced himself as Investigator Davis.

He began interrogating me and wanted to why I attempted to steal that light?" I was shaking and stuttering and told him because I didn't have enough money. He said, "Why didn't you ask your parents for the money?" I told him because I sold drink bottles and picked up pecans to raise the money to buy it myself. This was something I wanted to do. I was the only kid who didn't have one on their bike and I wanted a light. I could tell that he was touched by my words because he just stared at me and shook his head, He then gave me a long stern speech about my bad choices and where I was headed if I kept making them. He sat back in his chair for a moment. His next words surprised me. He said "Since it's your first time, I'm not sending you to the Youth Detention Center, but next time, I won't go easy on you. You understand?" I told him I did and promised to do right. I was so relieved. I would be able to get out of there without anyone knowing, I thought.

"Can you tell me where my bike is? He said, you can't leave by yourself you have to call someone to get you."

He then picked up the phone and asked, "Who should I call? What's their number?"

I thought about giving him a fake number, but I was already in trouble for being dishonest.

You can call "Big Mama and Big Daddy," I replied softly and then told him their phone number. Of all the people I didn't want to find out, it was my grandparents. They were wealthy and always provided for us. My grandfather had worked for the Central Georgia Railroad and was involved in a bad accident in Dawson, Georgia, where a train car box tipped over and fell on him. Fortunately, he fell into a deep ditch, which kept it from crushing him completely. Although he had to be dug out, he survived.

News reports say it was a miracle he came out alive. I still remember seeing him in a body cast for a long time after the incident. As a result, he received a large settlement. My grandparents were also well-respected in the community and didn't want our family name to be tarnished. I didn't want to embarrass them, but here I was, sitting in the police station, waiting for them to pick me up.

Big Daddy was mild-mannered, but Big Mama was sterned. She was a Byrd. That is her maiden name and boy didn't they make lots of noise. She had a way with words. She said what she meant and meant what she said. No filters, no compassions, no apologies, and no regrets. Whoever said, "Sticks and stones can break your bones, but words will never hurt you," didn't know my Big Mama. She would put "Madea to shame.

My grandparents arrived in about thirty minutes to pick me up. She apologized to Investigator Davis and assured him he would never, ever see me again. What did that mean? I thought to myself. Would I be better off serving my time in jail? They shook hands and he gave us my bike, and we were on our way.

When we got home, Big Mama put her pocketbook down and said "I feel like beating the hell out of you. You better not ever let me hear of you doing anything like this again or I will "light" your "_____" up. I said yes maam, I promised I won't ever do it again.

She then reached inside her purse and said here is some money go buy you a light. I started crying because of her love and compassion for me. Even though we make mistakes, we have a loving father who truly loves, forgives, and has compassion on us.

It is of the LORD's mercies that we are not consumed,
because his compassions fail not.
They are new every morning: great is thy faithfulness.
Lamentations 3:22-23

As I got older, I realized that my "light" ordeal was the beginning of my search for the true light of the world, Jesus Christ.

A few months later, I convinced my grandparents to allow me to move in with them and my aunt Diane permanently. I wanted to avoid peer pressure to do wrong, but most of all, I desired the peace, power, and prosperity of living with them. Their home also helped me escape other frightening situations.

There were a couple of guys who lived nearby that we kids avoided at all costs. One was a grown man who spent his time playing with kids. He would make inappropriate comments that made us question his motive. Word on the street was that he was a pedophile. The other guy was someone we called Bear because he was a big man with a deep voice and large nostrils. He had mental issues that no one talked about.

We were all scared of him. When someone saw him coming, they would yell, "Bear's coming!" and everyone scattered. If we were on the playground, we would run into the nearest house and lock the doors. We didn't want to mess around with him. Unbeknown to us at the time, he never harmed anyone. It was our ignorance and labels other people put on him that frightened us. I came to learn that he was a nice and gentle man who just wanted some friends.

3

CHAPTER

Loved Lost

I was in my last year of middle school at Merry Acres Middle School on the day my name was called over the school intercom. The secretary asked my teacher to send me to the office. I didn't know what was up. When I got to the office, my grandparents were there.

"Come on, let's go," Big Mama said.

"Where are we going?" I asked.

"We're going to the hospital. Your brother's been shot." Most everyone called him "Snoop." A well-known athlete in the community, he excelled at baseball in high school and was also known in our neighborhood as someone you didn't want to mess with. I liked that because it meant I was untouchable. I heard thugs in the community say about me, "Don't mess with him. That's Snoop's brother."

My grandparents and I stopped to pick up my sisters and mother. When we arrived at the hospital, he was in the Intensive Care Unit. Earlier in the day, Snoop had been hanging out with a friend at his house when the friend said he was showing him a gun when accidentally fired, and my brother was shot. At the hospital, people were donating blood to try to save his life, but to no avail. He died a few hours later. He was nineteen years old. My brother's friend served time in prison for murder.

Our family, friends, and the whole community were devastated. I cried for many days and nights. Not only was he my brother, but he was also my instructor and idol.

During his funeral arrangements my grandmother made it clear that it would not be held in any church. She believed that if you didn't walk into church, you shouldn't be rolled in one. My fourteen-year-old mind was reeling from her decision. To me, it meant that Snoop was going to hell. Fortunately, I found out later as I got older that I was solely mistaken. Snoop's eternal rest and entrance into heaven was not based on the location of his funeral but his accepting of the Lord as his personal savior.

There was an enormous crowd at my brother's funeral. The chapel was small so many people had to stand outside.

My family was never the same after that, especially my mother. She became very depressed and lost her will to live.. About five months later, my stepfather found her passed out on the floor. They called the ambulance and took her to the hospital. She had experienced a massive heart attack and died. I couldn't believe it. It was one of the most painful and grief-stricken periods of my life. It crushed my sisters and me. The mother who loved us and did her best for us during the good and bad times was now gone. What were three orphan kids going to do? We now only had each other and felt lost.

Unlike my brother's funeral, my grandmother allowed her memorial service to be held in a church sanctuary.

My mother's parents, sister Diane, and brother Lee, Jr., all contained their emotions very well. Although our stepfather cried quite a bit, it was nothing compared to the streams of tears, deep moans, and loud screams coming from the tender, broken hearts of her beloved three orphan kids: Belinda, Patricia, and me who was inconsolable.

A week after Mom's funeral, Big Mama reached out to our biological father because she didn't want my sisters to stay with our stepfather alone. After all, he wasn't responsible for raising any of us. However, our father wanted no part of it. He was living his own life and didn't want any interruptions. His exact words to her were, "I don't want them, do whatever you want to with them." Not only did he reject us, but he refused to make any provision for us financially, physically, or emotionally.

My dislike for him grew worse. If I had been older and bigger, I probably would have fought him for all the pain he caused us in the past and for the new pain of rejection he was inflicting on us. Even though he probably would have beaten my butt or even wounded me. Nevertheless, it would have been worth it to relieve my built-up resentment and rage. But in reality, I would have been fighting for his affection and validation that I so longed for.

Thankfully, my grandparents took in my sisters with us, and we never lacked for anything else again. Big Daddy and Big Mama instilled in us integrity, morals, and values that have protected us all of our lives and made us who we are today. They were the most caring, loving, and generous grandparents one could have. We will be forever thankful and indebted to them. It was nothing but God who touched their hearts and made a way for us to not become homeless. I can echo the words of King David when he said,

What shall I render unto the Lord for all his benefits?
I will take the cup of salvation, and call upon the name of the Lord. I will pay my vows unto the Lord now in the presence of all his people.
Psalm 116:12-14

Shortly after graduating from high school, my sister, Pat, moved to Cincinnati, Ohio, to live with our cousins, Jim and Beverly Byrd to attend college. My oldest sister, Belinda, stayed in Albany to work and raise her new baby boy, Joe "Nathan" Paige, Jr. I graduated the same year and immediately enlisted in the Army.

As soon as I received my first paycheck, I sent both money and continued to do so to help take care of them. It was the least I could do to show my concern for them.

4

CHAPTER

Put In A Pit

My first duty station was basic training in Fort Jackson, SC. Upon arrival our drill sergeant was waiting for us with a hostile look on his face. As soon as we exited the cattle truck he immediately started attacking and belittling us.

Five weeks into training, I'd had enough of the sergeant's verbal and mental abuse and decided to defy him. One morning I chose not to shave, and I knew it would make him extremely mad. We were lined up for the morning inspection, and the drill sergeant stopped in front of me and asked why I didn't shave. I told him because I didn't want to. He became very irate and started yelling and using obscenity.

Then he made me get into a 4 ft. pit outside the mess hall that was filled with cooking grease. It was dirty, stinky, slippery, and full of bugs. He handed me a small coffee cup and bucket and ordered me to clean it out using the cup to scoop out the grease and then pour it into the bucket. Once the bucket was full, I had to get out the pit and pour the grease into a large drum. This cycle was repeated until all the grease was gone. I wasn't allowed to take a break, eat, or drink anything until I was finished. It was a long and grueling task. I was completely exhausted when I left the pit. Nevertheless, the pit experience was therapeutic and symbolic of me clearing out all the damaging and undesirable things in my life.

Like Joseph in the Old Testament, many people have been put in a pit by someone else. Joseph's brothers threw him into a pit and then sold him into slavery. To me a pit is an early grave Satan digs for you in hopes he can bury you alive. Nevertheless, I realized no matter how I got there I didn't have to stay in that pit, and neither do you. God has made a way of escape and will lead you out of it. David said, in Psalm 40:1-3

"I waited patiently for the Lord, And He
inclined to me, and heard my cry.
He also brought me up out of a horrible pit, Out of the miry clay,
And set my feet upon a rock, And established
my steps. And he hath put
A new song in my mouth, even praise unto our God"

While the training was brutal and perhaps the hardest experience of my life, it also was one of the most pivotal experiences of my life because it was there that I met Zeke. Private Ezekiel "Zeke" Pettway made friends with everyone, even the less desirable soldiers. He was a great encouragement to me during those horrible weeks of training, and I came to appreciate him a great deal.

After basic training, we both received orders to go to A.I.T. - Advanced Individual Training Electronic Signal School at Fort Gordon, GA.

While stationed there we had more freedom, and most guys went to nightclubs on the weekends to party, pick up girls and whatever else wild soldiers did. I didn't want to be totally unsociable so one night I decided to hang out with them. I enjoyed the scenery and was a great dancer and loved the attention and applause I got for my moves. Our table was in the back corner where the guys were drinking and smoking weed. I wanted to be cool, so I took a couple of hits of what they were drinking. It wasn't very long before I started feeling woozy and began having a hard time talking and standing. Whether it was the weed, the alcohol, or both, I don't know. All I know was that I had never felt that way before. My friends started joking and making fun of me. We returned to the barracks, and I needed assistance getting to bed. The next morning, I felt horrible and vowed to never take a drink of alcohol again, and by the grace of God I haven't broken it.

My grandparents raised me up on the word of God, so instead of hanging out with the boys I started hanging out in the word. I found a Baptist church in Augusta where I started attending every week. I always invited the boys, especially Zeke to attend. Sometimes we would get into heated arguments after he had stayed out all night. Nevertheless, I was persistent and would not surrender to his cruel words and threats of violence. To God be the glory, today he is one of the most prolific, intellectual preachers and master orators in Montgomery, Alabama.

After A.I.T., I was stationed at Fort Bragg, NC, where I spent the remainder of my military career. It was also a place of transformation for me as the Holy Spirit began to do a new work in me.

I began to hunger and thirst for more knowledge and understanding of the word, so I started attending a Wednesday night Bible study. I vividly remember during one of those sessions the Holy Spirit spoke words to me that changed my life forever. We were reading the book of 2nd Corinthians 6:17-18 where it says:

"Wherefore, come out from among them, and be ye separate,"
saith the Lord, "and touch not the unclean thing; and I will
receive you. And will be a Father unto you, and ye shall
be my sons and daughters, saith the Lord Almighty."

I heard Him say to me stop tolerating and participating in worldly activities. I have called you out from among them. You are not only a soldier in the United States Army, but you have been recruited and now enlisted as a soldier in Army of the Lord.

But there was more. God said, "I will be your father and you my son". I started crying and rejoicing. The people didn't know what was happening, but I was thankful to finally know and experience the love of a father. I returned home that evening and reflected on those words over and over again.

Falling to my knees I opened my arms wide and embraced the sensation of being accepted by my heaven father. It was the beginning of a new spiritual season for me.

God had captured my heart and like the Apostle Paul, I was looking to apprehend the one who had apprehended me.

After four years of service, I was honorably discharged from the military and returned home. I had served my country for four years, and now I was beginning a lifetime of service to God.

5

CHAPTER

Answering The Call

When I returned home to Albany, I lived with my grandparents for a short time until I could find a job. It wasn't long before I was hired by the Albany Fire Department as a firefighter.

Living with my grandparents meant I was expected to attend the family church I grew up in. They were very influential leaders and required our participation in ministry. Their style of worship was very formal and totally different from the one I attended in North Carolina where the people were free worshippers. They sang, shouted, danced, ran, and praised God with all their might.

I shared my experience and passion with my grandparents who was very understanding and release me to follow my heart to worship wherever God leads me.

After a short time, I joined the Greater 2nd Mt. Olive Baptist Church under the leadership of Pastor C.W. Heath. I immediately became active and joined the senior usher board, men's ministry, and mass choir.

During that time, I began to sense God was calling me to preach. I want to be honest, but not heartless. Preaching was not part of my plans, I never inquired or desired to do it. Nevertheless, I couldn't deny what was happening. Like Jacob, I was in a wrestled with God and lost.

I shared my heart with two people who was close to me and would give me words of wisdom. The first was with my fiancé, Deirdere Goodman. I wanted her to know that if we were to continue our relationship it would most likely involve ministry. After sharing with her my sense of direction from the Lord, she was more than willing to stay with me. It was a very defining moment in our lives and relationship.

The other person was with my mentor and future pastor, Rev Daniel Simmons. He was serving as pastor of Pleasant Grove Baptist Church in Shingler, GA. and God led me there to sit under his tutoring. On May 21, 1989, I preached my first sermon titled "Who Side Are You On?" I served as his assistant for several years until he was called as the new pastor of Mt. Zion Baptist Church.

In November 1992, I was appointed pastor of Mountain Grove Baptist Church in Herod, GA. In May 1994, I was appointed pastor of New Saint James Baptist Church in Worth County, Ga. I served bi-weekly as pastor of both flock until I assumed the role as full time pastor of New Saint James in 1996.

On May 14, 1994, Deirdere and I married, and she assumed the role of First Lady.

Our son, Joshua Theophilus Smith, was born on March 16, 1995. We were elated to be new parents and thrilled about leading a thriving growing church.

While those days were exciting times of growth, God was doing something deep within me that would solidify the foundation of my life and faith. He was healing my heart of brokenness that I didn't want to face. But the time had finally come to confront it.

6

CHAPTER

Facing My Father

My dad had experienced some health problems for a while. While my sisters kept check on him and supplied his needs, I wanted no part of it. I just wanted him to suffer and feel the pain he caused us for so many years. The same words he said to my grandparents concerning the welfare of my sisters and I when we needed him, are the same words I repeat concerning him, "I don't care what happened to him".

Lots of bad memories flooded my mind pertaining to him such as his harsh treatment, lack of affection, lack of validation, lack of quality time, lack of fun times, lack of his present. His mental and physical abuse, the many days without electrical power, enough food and clothes, not coming home for days and especially the night he pointed his gun in my direction were things I replayed in my mind over and over again. I wanted revenge. Please don't judge me!

I know my action or lack thereof was wrong, but like the man in the bible who was on his way to Jericho, I had been robbed, stripped, wounded and left half dead. Many people who knew my condition turned their heads and passed by. It wasn't until many years later until the good Samaritan met me where I was, bound up my wounds, poured oil on me, took care of me. Luke 10:30-34

During his latter days in the hospital the Holy Spirit spoke to me and said, "No matter what he did or did not do, he is still your father, and you must forgive him." Now I was angry with God because this wasn't fair. Nevertheless, no matter how much I pouted he stood firm on his word.

"Honour thy father and mother; which is the
first commandment with a promise;
that it may be well with thee, and thou mayest live long on the earth."
Ephesians 6:2-3

Eventually, I swallowed my pride and visited him. He was in ICU on life support and couldn't say anything. For once, I was able to say what I wanted without any fear. The flood gate opened, and I was able to release everything that was damned up since I was a child. It was a very liberating and emotional time for both of us. His emotions activated an alarm, and a nurse quickly entered the room and consoled both of us, even though she didn't know the reason why we were crying. I never thought that day would come, but God is faithful.

The next few weeks of his life were very challenging for both of us. According to the doctors his organs were shutting down and we would soon have to make the decision to remove him off the ventilator.

For so many years, I did not want to be nowhere near him, but now I don't want to leave his side. Finally, the day, hour, minute and second came, when I watched the nurse slowly decrease the ventilator oxygen. It was one of the most horrendous and poignant experiences in my life.

I held his hand tightly and watched as she continued to turn the ventilator completely off. She nodded her head to let me know he was completely off life support and exited the room. His breathing was very slow and shallow until there was no sound heard. Oh No! He can't be gone, I thought to myself, we just began to connect as father and son. I could no longer bear it and hold back my tears. I laid my head on his chest for the first time in my life and wept. As a child, I always wanted to lie on him, but not under this condition.

A few weeks earlier I asked God to allow me to be the only person with him when he transitioned so I could endorse his parting. God answered my prayer, and I will cherish our last moments together for a lifetime. His funeral was celebratory, and I was elated to bury him in one of my most adored and expensive suits.

7

CHAPTER

The Fixed Fight

During one of the most thriving seasons of New Saint James Baptist Church era God told me it was time to build a new sanctuary. I was very elated to receive the vision and share our new venture with the congregation. After doing so, they seemed ecstatic and were in agreement with starting the project. I appointed a committee to start searching for land for the possibility of the new location. We had many families who were driving a distance, and I thought it would be helpful for them if we were closer to the city. It wasn't a definite plan, but something we were considering. We located nineteen acres of land for sale and began discussing our ideas with a real estate company.

During our first conversation the realtor told me she would check with the landowners and get back to me. When I didn't hear from her in a couple of weeks, I called her again. She told me she had spoken to the landowners who were now residing in Atlanta, Ga. and didn't want to sell it. It was designated for hunting wildlife as they often do. However, they assured her they would contact her if they ever decided to sell it. Several weeks later, I was working in my office at Procter & Gamble when the Holy Spirit spoke to me and said, "leave and drive to the land now." I immediately did so, and upon arrival He told me to get out and walk toward the realtor large "FOR SALE" sign. As I got closer to it, he told me to look down directly underneath it. To my surprise, I saw a small white sign covered up with weeds that had grown over it. I kneeled so I could see what was on it. There was a phone number on it that was faded by the weather and barely visible. I slowly wrote it down and headed back to work.

Upon my return I called the number, and when the person answered, I introduced myself and told him the reason for my call. His first words to me were, "How did you get my number?" After sharing the means, he told me he put the small sign there to advertise the land himself before placing it on the market, and the realtor company was supposed to have removed it. I apologized for calling and told him what the realtor said concerning his lack of interest in selling the land. He was flabbergasted. After gaining his composure, he told me he hadn't spoken with the realtor since it was put on the market about a year ago. Furthermore, he didn't live in Atlanta, nor did he hunt. Now, both of us were baffled. Why did she lie? Did she have an ulterior motive? One thing I do know is the enemy will use anybody to try blocking your blessing. We continued our conversation, and he said he purchased the 19 acres for his daughter to build a home, but she changed her mind, so he decided to sell it for $275,000.

I told him that I couldn't afford it and wished me success in my endeavor. I hung up the phone in dismay and went back to my work.

Several days later, he called me back and invited me to his home which was located next to land for sale. I inquired about the reason for my visit, and he said he would share it upon my I arrival.

He said God had spoken to him about selling me the land, and he was willing to make me another offer. However, I had to accept it right immediately and agree to build a church only on the property. I concurred, and he offered to sell it to me for only $90,000. That was a $185,000 reduction from his original offer, and it was less than what he had paid for it! This blessing reminded me of the words of the Apostle Paul in Ephesians 3:20:

Now unto Him who is able to do exceeding abundantly above all that we ask or think, according to the power that worketh in us.

This scripture became more real to me than it ever had before. Not only had God supplied our need, but He had exceeded it. I accepted the owner's offer, and we purchased the land shortly thereafter.

There's another beautiful twist to the story related to the name of the generous landowners. Their names were Mr. Will & Sara Grace. You read that right. Their last name was "Grace." That's exactly what God had showed me, "GRACE". So, what is grace? I'm glad you asked. It is defined as a special favor or privilege, a "disposition to or an act or instance of kindness, courtesy, or clemency." Grace is most often used in the Bible to refer to God's favor, "unmerited, divine assistance given to humans for their regeneration or sanctification." One of my favorite scriptures is:

But by the grace of God, I am what I am, and His grace toward
me was not in vain; but I labored more abundantly than they
all, yet not I, but the grace of God which was with me.
1 Corinthians 15:10, NIV

I was excited by the opportunity this new location would provide for my congregants and the community. Only God could have made this happen for us. After all, it looked like a red sea situation, a way was provided for us to get through to the other side. I was on top of the world from this blessing, but all of that was about to change dramatically.

It wasn't long before the idea of moving was leaked to the congregation, and many of them became very upset. Before long, the furor grew, and "delirious" is a nice way of describing their response. We called a meeting to give people a chance to share their feelings and why they were so frantic about the possibility of moving.

We scheduled the meeting early one Saturday morning. It was an extremely cold and misty morning and the first time everyone was on time for church. My good friend, Pastor Ezekiel "Zeke" Pettway, came from Alabama to support. My wife and young son were also with me as he drove us to New Saint James Baptist Church for the meeting. The sanctuary was filled to capacity as people came from everywhere to witness this much-anticipated hearing. I was concerned about how the meeting would go but was assured God was on our side. The chairman of deacons opened the meeting with prayer and the order of business. However, before he could get very far, he was rudely interrupted, and the meeting quickly spun out of control immediately. His effort to regain command and calm was for nought, so I motioned him to take his seat and allow them to speak. I don't have words to describe their level of immoral and inhumane conduct they displayed in the house of God. Several were armed and ready for battle. They had strategized their mode of operation and revealed themselves as pure hypocrites. Instead of having a reasonable conversation and coming to a peaceful resolution as Christians, they did otherwise. Some used vile, despicable, vulgar, hateful, hostile and threating language in their insults and attacks. Again, this was inside the temple of God, they were behaving as roaring lions, and I was their prey. I was mauled and called everything they could conceive including false preacher, cult leader, fraud, lucifer, deranged and the "N" word, just to name a few. They accused me of stealing money, paying personal bills, cheating, deception, family members benefits and many more disgusting things that I rather not regurgitate. One lady told me she would spend everything she had to see my head on a platter "behead" me like John the Baptist. All those things were psychotic, but the most bizarre and frightening words was when a gentleman said he visited the church's cemetery last night and had a conversation with the dead. They told him to speak up and vote for them against relocating or building a new church. This was "the straw that broke the camel's back" for me. It was the jarring, jaw dropping and defining moment for me to get my family out of there and run as fast as we could. Even though God had given me peace through it all, it felt like I had been to hell and back.

During their rants and raging, like Jesus, I never said a murmuring word. The words of the Prophet Isaiah was my solace.

Thou wilt keep him in perfect peace, whose mind is
stayed on thee: because he trusteth in thee.
Isaiah 26:3, KJV

In anticipation it would be a chaotic meeting, I sought a solution that transcended human wisdom and intervention. It was then that the idea of inviting intercessors was conceived. They were people whose sole responsibility was to pray before, during, and after the meeting, seeking divine intervention. The intercessors were ladies of deep faith, known for their unwavering belief in the power of prayer. In the days leading up to the meeting they dedicated themselves to prayer and fasting, seeking God's presence and asking for His will to prevail.

The prayers of the intercessors weaved a tapestry of calm within our lives as we marched forth toward our promised land. The intercessors were under the majestic leadership of Prophetess Patricia Davis and Prophetess Gwen Redding. Their intercessory team included Elect Lady Deirdere Smith, Lizzie Reid, Pamela May, Belinda Smith, Sharon Sumbry, Roshonda Kendrick, Kimberly Macon, Verleta Reid, Connie Reid, Belinda Thomas, Darlene Fowler, Charlotte Terrell, and Monica Carter.

After assuring everyone who opposed me had spoken, I requested a vote on moving forward with the project, and the majority voted to abandon it. My only words to them were God said, "You did not reject me, but you rejected Him, and this ground is cursed." I then called my friend, Zeke, to pray and give the benediction. You would have thought it was all over, but you're wrong. This debacle was just the beginning of a relentless battle that would continue to rage on in unprecedented ways.

8

CHAPTER

Barred From Going Back

The drive home from the meeting was dismal. It felt like we were leaving a funeral after the final words were spoken and the body was lowered into the ground—only this time, I felt like I was the person buried. Zeke drove us back to my home. It was a quiet ride with few words being spoken. I was deflated and done. The level of hostility was far more than I had anticipated. I had served as their pastor for six years, and they had always listened and followed my lead. But now, in just a few hours, all of that trust and support had disappeared. Tears of sorrow rolled down my face, revealing the pain I was feeling all through my body. All I say was, "Father, if thou be willing, remove this cup from me: nevertheless, not my will, but thine, be done."

After we arrived home, Zeke stayed, and we talked for a while. Before he left but promised that as I had been with hm and stayed by his side while he fought his internal personal demons, he would stand with me while I fought my external religious demons. The power of friendship is a lesson I've learned over the years. Many people think they don't need anyone else but let me assure you there will come a time when you need all the help you can get. The devil and his ranks of demons will attack in ways you never expected, and without a "battle buddy," you will certainly be defeated. We find this wisdom in Ecclesiastes 4:9-12 (NLT).

Two people are better off than one, for they can help each other succeed. If one person falls, the other can reach out and help. But someone who falls alone is in real trouble. Likewise, two people lying close together can keep each other warm. But how can one be warm alone? A person standing alone can be attacked and defeated, but two can stand back-to-back and conquer. Three are even better, for a triple-braided cord is not easily broken.

One of the main reasons Jesus sent out his disciples in pairs was because of this very idea. He knew they would face the enemy because of the nature of their mission. A companion would give them additional strength to stand against the opposition in their togetherness. He said to them,

Behold, I send you forth as lambs among wolves.

I'll point out that wolves don't just damage their prey. They totally demolish them. If you decide to face battles alone, expect the same. Our adversary is a powerful force to be reckoned with, and we would be wise to follow Jesus's example and invite others to fight with us rather than face him alone. One of the main reasons many lives have been destroyed is because they were too prideful to ask for help. First comes pride, and then comes a crash. It's inevitable.

After the meeting, I was perplexed about what to do. I invited a guest speaker for Sunday morning. I decided that I should resign from New St. James Baptist Church because I could no longer lead the people. I wanted to handle it according to the scripture, "Let all things be done decently and in order," but these people thrived in chaos. I met with the building committee and told them of my plans to resign. I also told them that God told me to continue the process of building a new church. Within a few days, I received a letter from an attorney representing the church ordering me to disband the building committee and cease all construction plans. I was surprised they had gone to the expense of involving a lawyer. But I shouldn't have been surprised since they were like the Pharisees and Sadducees, who would stop at nothing to halt Jesus. It was apparent they thought I was still planning to move forward with their building, but they were wrong. Since they hired an attorney, I retained one and turned everything over to him. I continued to invite other ministers to conduct their church services until I officially resigned. However, before I could do so, they dropped another bomb on me.

While working on my secular job (Procter & Gamble Paper Company), early one Tuesday morning I received a call from our head security officer to report to her office. She told me that there was a sheriff deputy at the main entrance gate who wanted to see me about a church matter. After sharing the troubling ordeal with her she teared up and encouraged me to stay the course. Then she informed the deputy that I would not be allowed to talk with him and asked him to leave immediately. This spectacle was orchestrated by a couple of female church members who worked there and wanted to embarrass me. Nevertheless, God had a merciful, compassionate and loving woman of God named Barbara Tillman to stand in the gap and destroy the plans of the enemy.

Not too many days later, to my surprise a deputy came to my home around 10pm one night. When I answered the door, he said he was there to serve me restraining order filed by several members of New Saint James Baptist Church. The order prevented me from operating as the pastor and returning onto the church property for any reason.

I was mystified but not surprised by their wickedness. Although I was still the pastor legally, I had no intention of continuing as their overseer. They feared so and were able to deceive a judge into issuing a restraining order.

FILED
WORTH COUNTY
CLERK'S OFFICE

-IN THE SUPERIOR COURT OF WORTH COUNTY
STATE OF GEORGIA

03 JAN 24 AM 10: 15

JOANN F. POWELL
CLERK

JOHNNIE JAMES, DEACON LONZIE :
JAMES, DEACON RICHARD LAKE, and :
DEACON NATHANIAL THOMAS, et al :

CIVIL ACTION FILE NO.

Plaintiffs,

vs.

___03 CV 20_____

RONALD SMITH, INDIVIDUALLY
AND IN HIS CAPACITY AS PASTOR
OF THE NEW ST. JAMES MISSIONARY :
BAPTIST CHURCH; PAMELA MAY, :
JOHN REID AND MELVIN FOWLER :

Defendants.

TEMPORARY RESTRAINING ORDER

Having found upon good cause shown that the instant Temporary Restraining Order must be executed ex parte due to the urgency of protecting the assets of the New Saint James Missionary Baptist Church, the Court hereby orders that Ronald Smith is temporarily restrained from acting in his capacity as Pastor of the New Saint James Missionary Baptist Church and from entering the church premises unless escorted by either Deacon Lonzie James, Deacon Richard Lake or Deacon Nathaniel Thomas. Further, Ronald Smith is hereby restrained from accessing any church property including bank accounts, vehicles, real property and personal property. The instant Temporary Restraining Order shall expire thirty (30) days from the date the instant Order is signed.

Georgia, Worth County
I certify that this is a true and complete
copy of the original which is on file in
the Clerk of Superior Courts office this

GARY CLINTON MCCORVEY, JUDGE
SUPERIOR COURT OF WORTH COUNTY

executed 8:56 A.M.
1-23-03

(Deputy Clerk) Superior Court

56

The legal action perplexed me. Why send restraining orders? The restraining order is a protection for someone who fears for their personal safety. If there was anyone who should have felt threatened, it was me. They didn't just stop with the restraining order. Later that month my lawyer was notified that some disgruntled church members had filed a civil lawsuit. They were holding me and others liable for illegal financial transactions and the deterioration of health that led to illness, injuries, and death of some church members. A few who opposed the vision God gave me became gravely ill and several died. They claimed it was due to stress and anxiety brought upon them by my administration and actions related to the building project.

However, in their haste to inflict more pain upon me, they fail to recall the last words spoken to them "You didn't reject me, but God and the church ground are cursed". The curse was manifesting itself in many ways among them and causing severe grief, but instead of repenting they were resisting.

My attorney responded to their lawsuit with the aggressiveness of a warrior. He told their attorney in no uncertain terms that if they didn't stop their stupidity, he would not only suit the church but their businesses, lawyer and members personally. He made it clear that the lawsuit and the restraining order were erroneous and a mockery of the court. Their attorney was terrified and quickly convinced his clients to withdraw their litigations. They agreed, and we both signed a release order from any future allegations. Finally, it was finally over, and I could move forward with what God told me to do.

What made this season of transition so baffling for me was what God spoke to me several years earlier while I was in my man cave. Throughout biblical times, God often spoke to men when they were in a cave. He started a divine movement through King David when he was held up in a cave.

> *David therefore departed thence, and escaped to the cave*
> *Adullam: and when his brethren and all his father's*
> *house heard it, they went down thither to him. And*
> *everyone that was in distress, and everyone that was in debt,*
> *and everyone that was discontented, gathered themselves*
> *unto him; and he became a captain over them:*
> *and there were with him about four hundred men.*
> 1 Samuel 22:1-2, KJV

A cave is the place where you usually hear God like never before. Some of my most sacred and divine revelations came when I was in a cave. Not just a physical one, but a spiritual cave. Often, I emerged as a very different person, spiritually, mentally, and emotionally. On this day, Like the Prophet Ezekiel, God showed me a vision of the future. In it I saw a configuration of a man who motioned me to follow him down a long corridor.

I followed him into a large open room where he placed his hands on my shoulders and turned me around to face him. He then told me to open my mouth and he put a door key inside and told me to swallow it. I expected to choke and regurgitate it, but not so. To my surprise it went down my throat with ease. I was shocked.

He told me to close my eyes and put my hands down to the side. Again, he placed his hands on my shoulders and turned my back to him. He told me to open my eyes, and when I did so there was a huge sanctuary. The sight was overwhelming, and I began to shake. I turned around to ask him what it meant, but he was no longer in sight. I looked up to heaven and asked God what it meant, and He said, "This is yours."

The key represents access to which you have authority to open new doors without any resistance or struggle. Everything in your future endeavors will be extremely easy. I was in awe. Suddenly, it was all over, and I came to myself crying and shaking my head wondering what had just happened. After regaining my composure, I continued my studies for a few more hours, then went about my daily routine, never speaking of it to anyone.

This is the main reason why I was bewildered about everything that happened. If the vision was prophetic, why was everything so difficult? This building had become the hardest experience of my life! Amid all the chaos, I was confused because God cannot lie. Early one morning around 3am. my doorbell rang. I wondered who it could be? Was it the police again? I didn't know and wasn't about to take any chances. I got out of bed, threw on some clothes and grabbed my pistol. At that moment, I was fed up and ready to take matters into my hands. I went to the door with my pistol behind my right leg.

I asked, "Who is it?" The person responded "Pastor! It's me, Adolph Kendrick." I opened the door and asked him what he was doing at my house this time of morning. He said, "I'm sorry to disturb you, but I couldn't sleep." "God told me to get up and come and tell you, 'Everything is going to be alright, and He's got your back".

I stood there and thought to myself, if you try this again, you're going to need him to have your back! Nevertheless, Adolph's visit was exactly what I needed at the time. God was reassuring me of his divine protection and all I needed to do was to trust Him.

There will be times on your journey, no matter your spiritual relationship, status or identity you will need encouragement. God will send someone at the right time (even at 3am) to inspire you to keep going. This was true for the Prophet Elijah and for me and you.

The bible says in 1 Kings 19:1-8

And Ahab told Jezebel all that Elijah had done, and withal how he had slain all the prophets with the sword. Then Jezebel sent a messenger unto Elijah, saying, So let the gods do to me, and more also, if I make not thy life as the life of one of them by tomorrow about this time. And when he saw that, he arose, and went for his life, and came to Beersheba, which belongeth to Judah, and left his servant there. But he himself went a day's journey into the wilderness, and came and sat down under a juniper tree: and he requested for himself that he might die; and said, It is enough; now, O LORD, take away my life; for I am not better than my fathers. And as he lay and slept under a juniper tree, behold, then an angel touched him, and said unto him, Arise and eat. And he looked, and, behold, there was a cake baken on the coals, and a cruse of water at his head. And he did eat and drink, and laid him down again. And the angel of the LORD *came again the second time, and touched him, and said, Arise and eat; because the journey is too great for thee. And he arose, and did eat and drink, and went in the strength of that meat forty days and forty nights unto Horeb the mount of God.*

1 Kings 19:1-8

My wife was constantly encouraging during this hard season, she reminded me of Romans 11:29, *God's gifts and his call are irrevocable.*

In other words, God's gifts, calls, and assignments are never canceled. Those words energized my soul. I felt more empowered and equipped to fulfill His plans for me. It was also a powerful learning time for me. The lesson that has stuck with me all these years is the reason for this book. It has had an unforgettable and profound impact on me ever since.

9

CHAPTER

God Served Restraining Orders

About a month later, the Holy Spirit moved me to read and study the 19th chapter of Genesis. I've preached from this chapter many times, so I was curious, "What di God wanted me to learn this time that I hadn't before?"

This chapter is primarily about the destruction of Sodom and Gomorrah because of sin. The people who lived there were committing sexual acts and other ungodly things without any remorse. However, before releasing His wrath upon them, God sent His angels to instruct a man named Lot and his family to depart from the cities. As a result of Lot's slothfulness and the urgency of the destruction, God's angels had to take his family by their hands and quickly usher them outside the cities to avoid death. When they had brought them out, one of the angels said to them,

> *Run for your life! Do not look behind you. Do*
> *not stop until you are out of the valley.*
> Genesis 19:17, NIV

To get them out of harm's way God removed and restrained them from the cities. Not only did he restrain them from going back but looking back. RUN FOR YOUR LIFE! They were not permitted to have any connection or inclination of returning to the place God vigorously brought them out. This must have been difficult for them because even though Sodom and Gomorrah were evil cities, it had also been their home for many years. They had raised their children there and had many friends.

When I read that part of the story, I was astonished. The Holy Spirit said, "Did you get it? "It wasn't the people in the city doing, but God who restrained Lot family from returning. I want you to clearly understand this fact; it wasn't the members of New Saint James Baptist Church, but God who served you and your family restraining orders. He wanted you out from among the impious, scoffers and blasphemers (Not all but the majority) of people. The time had come for God to release his judgement on them but would not do so until your family were out.

I shook my head in disbelief and said, "Say that again. Did I hear you correctly? Are you telling me it was God who sent the deputy to my home to serve me restraining orders?" "Yes, it was God! You left Him no choice. He had to send it to keep you from cooperating with the enemy and aborting the plans of God."

To say that I was speechless is an understatement. I was knocked to my knees and began to weep severely. It was a revitalizing and redefining moment in my life and ministry. I began to see everything from a different perspective.

In biblical times God allowed church conflict to occur as a way of relocating his people so they could accomplish their mission.

In the first three verses of Acts 8, we see that God allowed his church to experience a time of tribulation—hardship, inconvenience, fear, loss, shame, rejection, and abuse. The oppression was so great in Jerusalem that the members of the church had to pack up their things, their families, their lives, and seek safety. Some had grown up in Jerusalem. Some had family members they left behind. These people were being forced to relocate because of opposition and growing persecution.

While there was tribulation, there was also proclamation. While the church was enduring hardship, they were also unrelenting in their witness. The scattering of the church was done *to them*, but there's also a sense of intentionality to it—both on the part of the people of God and on the part of the God they serve. Yes, there was persecution. Yes, the church was passively being scattered. But, at the same time, God was actively using this persecution to mobilize his people to accomplish the assignment he'd given them early in life. God may have allowed his church to experience a time of tribulation, but He also used this time of tribulation to cause them to walk in their purpose. We must always remember that God is more concerned with our holiness than our happiness.

I began to search the scriptures and discovered God used the same method many times in the past. He served restraining orders to others to keep them from returning to their former place, occupation, and lifestyle. Abraham was restrained from returning to Haran, Ruth from Moab, Elisha from the field, Saul from Damascus, and David from the palace, just to name a few. We read of moments in Israel's history where He restrained them. When the nation went contrary to God's ways, He would use other countries as a rod of correction for His own people. A memorable moment in Israel's history occurred in 587 B.C. when He allowed Babylon to invade their borders and take them into captivity for 70 years. Were it not for the harsh treatment the people of Israel had to suffer, they would have never forsaken their choices.

This lesson of restraining orders seems to be the opposite of how most people think God operates. We tend to think God's blessings will be progressive and painless, and anything contrary is from the enemy. However, we forget that He regularly responds in the opposite way of how we expect and will allow things to go contrary to our conventional way of thinking.

> *"For my thoughts are not your thoughts, neither*
> *are your ways my ways," saith the Lord.*
> Isaiah 55:8, KJV

We see this lesson repeated throughout the scripture. For example, we read the story of Jesus's disciples traveling across the Sea of Galilee when a terrible storm suddenly arose, and they thought the boat would capsize and they would drown. They were terrified. But Jesus came to them in a way they never expected, walking on the tumultuous water through the wind and rain, speaking to them,

It is I; do not be afraid.

—John 6;20, KJV

The conditions of the storm had blurred their vision of Jesus, which is why they didn't know who he was. It's no different from where many people are today. Life's situations can blur our vision of Jesus. He's present, but we don't see him. Just as His presence and words changed their whole outlook of the storm, so did He change my outlook on my storm. It's a principle that gives us great comfort.

Once I received this new revelation, I was rejuvenated and invigorated more than ever. It gave me new energy, enthusiasm and resolve to keep on pushing forward.

God restrains us, His children, protecting us from ourselves and our misguided ways. His interventions in our lives are acts of love because He is a most loving Father.

For the Lord disciplines those he loves, and he punishes each one he accepts as his child. As you endure this divine discipline, remember that God is treating you as his own children. Who ever heard of a child who is never disciplined by its father?
Hebrews 12:6-7, NLT

The opposite of love is not hatred. I believe it is indifference. Most men who are incarcerated with whom I have talked said their fathers did not care about them. They let them do whatever they wanted. They weren't restrained and ended up hurting themselves and other people. As a result, they spent many years being restrained by someone else who didn't love them, which is much harder.

It was during my father's desertion that I attempted to steal the bicycle light from the store. Since he wasn't around to restrain me, God put other people in my life who did so. I can't thank my mother for doing her very best to restrain me. My grandparents were instrumental in restraining me with their presence and guidance. God also used the police to keep me from going down the wrong path. If I had gotten away with stealing the light, who knows the path I would have taken or where I would be today? The police investigator saw a young child who had made a poor decision, and rather than punishing me, he protected and restrained me from incarceration.

While that incident in the store was temporary, the effects were everlasting. It was a life transforming. I'm reminded of the words of the Apostle Paul who wrote;

> For the time being no discipline brings joy,
> but seems grievous *and* painful;
> but afterwards it yields a peaceable fruit of righteousness
> to those who have been trained by it [a harvest of fruit
> which consists in righteousness—in conformity to
> God's will in purpose, thought, and action, resulting
> in right living and right standing with God].
> Hebrews 12:11 Amplified

Discipline is one of the greatest expressions of love. We fear that the other person will be hurt and think we don't love them. That's the card children will often play when they are being disciplined. They will claim their parents don't love them. However, the opposite is true. Restraining someone from their own choices shows you do care about what happens to them.

You love them greatly and want only good for them, so you restrain them from the harm and damage they will face if they aren't restrained. God, our Father, is like this. He restrains us because He loves us and wants what is best for us.

One way God restrains us is in the relationships we build. We are tempted to build and hold onto relationships with people whose faith, values, and vision don't align with ours. This connection can include a friendship, relationship, marriage, or business partner. God has a great plan for our lives and will not allow a perpetrator to disrupt that plan.

10
CHAPTER

Time Of Transition

One of the greatest lessons I've learned in life is that many of our important relationships have a season. Solomon, one of the wisest men in history, wrote:

> *To everything, there is a season, and a time to every purpose under the heaven: A time to be born, and a time to die; a time to plant, and a time to pluck up that which is planted; A time to kill, and a time to heal; a time to break down, and a time to build up; A time to weep, and a time to laugh; a time to mourn, and a time to dance.*
>
> Ecclesiastes 3:1-4, NIV

We will have relationships in our spiritual journey here on earth with two types of people: those who are *"called to us"* and those who are *"called through us."* Those who are called to us are people whose very calling in life is to work and walk with us to the finish line. They have the same type of spiritual DNA and are just as passionate about the things we care about. They gladly share in our vision for the future. An example of this type of relationship is our spouses, children, brothers, sisters, spiritual sons and daughters, and covenant partners. People may come and go, but those who are spiritually ordained and connected are bound by the covenant to stay with us to the finish line. There are many who are reading this book who know who are. You've been sent by God to serve along beside me until eternity. My words to you are the same as the Prophet Elijah spoke to Elisha:

When they reached the other side, Elijah said to Elisha;
"What can I do for you before I'm taken from you? Ask anything."
Elisha said, "Your life repeated in my life. I want to be a holy
man just like you." "That's a hard one!" said Elijah. "But if
you're watching when I'm taken from you, you'll get what
you've asked for. But only if you're still with me watching."
2 Kings 2:9-10

On the other hand, people *"called through us"* are in the majority. These are individuals who will work and walk with us in our spiritual journey toward our prophetic destiny for a certain time. Some start out with us and then move on at some point in our prophetic journey. Others join us halfway to our destiny, while others yoke with us at the tail end of our spiritual journey. We must allow everybody to be a blessing to our ministry during their allotted time of destiny and then send them with a blessing when their spiritual season expires.

God is a God of purpose. Everything He does is done for a purpose. God only brings people into our lives in the spirit of purpose. Once those people have fulfilled God's purpose for being with us, God will instigate a time of transition to move them out of our lives. It's a restraining order. He's restraining us from them and them from us. In most cases, these people will suddenly lose the spiritual passion they once had for our vision and become more and more distracted and disheartened.

Our problem is that instead of recognizing this period as a divinely orchestrated time of transition, we do everything humanly possible to hold on to the relationship. So much so that we will bargain with the enemy, which will eventually lead to sin. At this point, we find ourselves on the wrong side of the law of transition, and when this happens, things can get messy.

We quickly discover that the people who had been a blessing to us in the past have now become a pain in the neck because we have forced them to overstay their season of purpose. By the time we finally decide to let them go, what was left of the relationship is in ruins. This normally happens because the flesh loves to hold on to things, even when it is getting nothing in return. It's our failure to perceive their breaking away as an expression of God's restraining orders that creates the problems that arise. Once we understand the value of these transitions, we will not lose relationships with people when their season to move on comes. We must spiritually mature as adults to the point where we can celebrate people's entry into our lives as well as their exit, especially when we know that the Lord's hand is in it. Why should we demonize people once they exit our lives when they have given us many years of fruitful service in the past? This is immature, inaccurate, and improper behavior.

Every relationship on the planet has an expiration date on it, even the ones with our wives and family. The day came when Solomon had to let go of his father, King David, as he passed into eternity. David's wife, Bathsheba, also had to let him go. This is life. It's no big mystery, and yet thousands of people in our world fail to successfully handle transitions in relationships.

Jesus himself rebuked his disciples for grieving when He told them that He was going to leave so the Holy Spirit could take His place.

> But now I go my way to him that sent me; and none of you asketh me, Whither goest thou? But because I have said these things unto you, sorrow hath filled your heart. Nevertheless, I tell you the truth; It is expedient for you that I go away: for if I go not away, the Comforter will not come unto you; but if I depart, I will send him unto you. And when he is come, he will reprove the world of sin, and of righteousness, and of judgment.
>
> John 16:5-8, NIV

Jesus knew His season of ministry with the disciples here on earth was coming to an abrupt end, so He began to talk more with them about the Holy Spirit than He spoke of Himself. He knew their next level of ministry was not with Him but with the Holy Spirit, which is why He was leaving.

This is a serious statement for us to consider because it reveals the power of transition in a very striking way.

What Jesus was saying to the disciples was simply this, "I have to obey the law of transition; otherwise, the Holy Spirit will never come to the earth and dwell among you!" It was a restraining order. Even for Jesus, transition was the surest and most effective way of closing one spiritual season to enter another!

During periods of transition, bad things may happen to godly people, but this is no reason to turn away from the call of God upon our lives. One of the greatest dangers during times of transition is aborting our prophetic destiny because of misinterpreting the attacks of the enemy upon our lives. More often than not, the enemy's onslaught should be an indication that we are closer to seizing our breakthrough than we have ever been. This is why believers and people of faith must learn the benefits of suffering for the cause of Christ while doing the will of God rather than thinking that every problem indicates they missed God!

Some believers in Christ who have been raised in "word of faith churches" sometimes suffer from this type of spiritual delusion by leaders who don't rightly divide the word. Please don't misunderstand me. I am not against word-of-faith churches, prosperity churches, or any other type of church. However, I am against the spiritual practice of focusing on prosperity scriptures while ignoring those that say we are called to suffer even as Christ suffered. I believe we must take the Bible in its entirety and not pick and choose the scriptures that say what we want to hear.

There is a tendency by some proponents of the prosperity message to use a man's material possessions as evidence of God's divine approval. At the same time, any form of spiritual turbulence in one's life is frowned upon as a sign of divine disapproval! This great deception can force us into a compromise during times of difficult transition.

During periods of transition, we may be tempted to speak evil of people and places we used to be a part of, but we must resist this temptation. Such unbecoming behavior can abort the prophetic destiny God has for us!

Transitions are a part of life. Our efforts to fight against them are futile. Instead, we can learn to embrace them as God's restraining orders and move forward. Our destiny awaits, and only as we choose to let go of that which we can't hold will we walk into the purposes of God.

11

CHAPTER

The Seven Saints Of Satan

Even though I was relieved and had peace knowing God had served me the restraining orders, and not the opposing church members or even the judge, I was still furious about the malicious ways my family and other faithful members were mistreated. Determined to get even, I began contemplating ways to get revenge on them, especially a specific group known as "The Seven Saints of Satan." I honestly felt they were demonic possessed because of their uncontainable violent and vicious attacks. They did everything human possible to destroy me and make my life a living hell. Now that the ball was in my court, I felt it was time for them to reap what they sowed.

However, I didn't want them to suffer to the same degree, but much worse. As a Christian, I know the Bible instructs us to overcome evil with good, but I felt it was justified. Since they started it, I was going to finish it.

Nonetheless, before I could lay out my plans with my accomplices, the Holy Spirit intervened and convicted me. He reminded me of his word:

Do not say, "Thus I shall do to him as he has done to me;
I will render to the man according to his work."
Proverbs 24:29, KJV

Beloved, never avenge yourselves, but leave it to the wrath of God,
for it is written, "Vengeance is mine, I will repay," says the Lord.
Romans 12:19, NKJV

I thought to myself, "this isn't right". Why should they get away with all they've done. My understanding of why Jonah was upset and fled in the opposite became more apparent. Like Jonah, I was mad with God and in no mood to wait for Him to punish them for their ill treatment toward me and others with me. Why was He protecting them? After all, they started, and I was ready to finish it.

In my displeasure, I went outside to my man cave and isolated myself from everyone. Later that evening, my wife came out and wanted to know what was bothering me. I told her, but she was not sympathetic. Instead, she asked me one question, "What Would Jesus Do?" In my phrenzy, I said, "I don't care what He would do; he hasn't been hurt like me." She looked straight at me and said, "You're right, He wasn't, but a whole lot worse.

He was killed, you're still living". "You need to get yourself together and let God handle them." Then she walked out. Now I was mad at her for speaking the truth. Her words pierced my heart like a javelin, and deflated everything I was holding inside.

One of my favorite scriptures I often quote and share with others who are harboring anger is:

Be not hasty in thy spirit to be angry: for
anger resteth in the bosom of fools.
Ecclesiastes 7:9,

That's exactly why I was acting like a fool. I finally surrendered my will to God's will concerning this matter. It was only then I realized it was part of the devil's scheme to not only embarrass and hurt me, but my entire family. God is the righteous judge and decides the avenged outcome of every injustice. There's never a fitting time to seek revenge because He will always bring about justice for His people. We can trust that when we are wronged or hurt by others, God knows the details and will avenge us in His time. We may not understand why God never punishes the wicked instantly but allows them to live or even prosper in their evil schemes. But one thing you must understand as Isaiah 55:8,9 tells us is that God's thoughts are not our thoughts neither are His ways our ways nor do we have God's perfect knowledge and understanding to understand why He does certain things. Moreover, you need to understand that just because the wicked are not punished immediately doesn't mean they won't face divine punishment and judgment for their iniquity eventually.

When we take matters into our own hands, we make things worse for ourselves and others. That's why He restrains us from revenge. He's protecting us because He loves us.

Many people asked me, "Did this ordeal ever make me think about quitting ministry?" Absolutely not! The Apostle Paul was a man who severely suffered while during ministry, yet it was his pain that kept him pushing.

> *And now, behold, I go bound in the spirit unto Jerusalem,*
> *not knowing the things that shall befall me there: Save that*
> *the Holy Ghost witnesseth in every city, saying that bonds*
> *and afflictions abide me. But none of these things move me,*
> *neither count I my life dear unto myself, so that I might finish*
> *my course with joy, and the ministry, which I have received*
> *of the Lord Jesus, to testify the gospel of the grace of God.*
> Acts 20:23-24 KJV

When face to face with overwhelming and offensive opposition, Jesus refused to quit His calling. With His life on the line and time ticking away, Jesus pressed forward and stayed the course, suffered the cross, and bought our salvation. If He could endure such unspeakable betrayals, then surely we can face the challenges that come our way without quitting. He is our perfect example.

> *Looking unto Jesus the author and finisher of our faith; who for*
> *the joy that was set before him endured the cross, despising the*
> *shame, and is set down at the right hand of the throne of God.*
> Hebrews 12:2, NIV

Ministry, like much of life, does not take place in constant excitement. It is often a ritual or a routine that can be dull, deadly, and dark at times. Some days, just showing up requires a heroic effort! There are seasons of hard and uneventful work for the cause of Christ. During these challenges, we are taunted with ideas to abandon our work, that we are fighting a losing battle, and that our efforts are futile. But still, we must fight on.

We must lash ourselves to the Word of God and refuse to let the temptation of compromise deflect us from our God-assigned ministry. No matter how difficult the situation or brutal the warfare, we must constantly affirm that quitting is not an option because God has empowered us to persist. When we do, we discover that perseverance brings forth abundant joy and greater fruitfulness, more than we can imagine.

If thou faint in the day of adversity, thy strength is small.
Proverbs 24:10

12

CHAPTER

Shake It Off

Even though it was one of the most arduous times in my life, I am confident that God was equipping me for a greater work that would require a deeper and stronger foundation.

I knew what God was directing me to do, so I immediately began searching for a place to start the new church. The location I found was Thronateeska Heritage Center, 100 W. Roosevelt Avenue. I met with my new leadership team, and we agreed to launch the ministry on January 19, 2003. We notified those who were interested in joining us and invited them to service. There were about 93 people in attendance. The title of the first sermon was "Shake the Dust Off Your Feet." The same message Jesus told his disciples:

> *And whosoever shall not receive you, nor hear your words, when*
> *ye depart out of that house or city, shake off the dust of your feet.*
> Matthew 10:14, NIV

Shaking the dust off one's feet is a symbolic indication that one has done all that can be done in a situation and, therefore, carries no further responsibility for it. In the scriptural examples,

Jesus was telling His disciples that they were to preach the Gospel to everyone. Where they were received with joy, they should stay and teach, but where their message was rejected, they had no further responsibility.

They were free to walk away with a clear conscience, knowing they had done all they could do. There are times when God gives us the freedom to move on. We figuratively "shake the dust off our feet" when, under the Holy Spirit's direction, we surrender those people to the Lord and emotionally let go.

For the people of Berachah Church, this message meant it was time for us to let go of the past and move forward. Some emotional and spiritual wounds needed to heal from the situation and the time for healing had come.

We devised a way by which we could symbolically break all ties. I requested everyone bring all items; clothing, photographs, choir robes, bulletins or anything else related to the NSJ to church the following week. We set up two barrels and put those items inside and burned them. It was therapeutic and liberating for all in attendance. We shouted and praised God for His mighty acts.

13

CHAPTER

After Hours and Back Door Blessings

After one year operating as a new ministry, God said it was time to move forward and build the church as He commanded two years earlier. With new orders, I began compiling the church's financial records into a portfolio. I selected three banks to apply for a commercial construction loan. My time with the first two banks loan officers was very brief because I didn't have the information and documents required which includes: 3 to 5 years of history, collateral, credit, debt service ratio, profit and loss statements, balance sheets, and most importantly, a good down payment. Even though their response was negative, I kept a positive attitude. When God gives a vision, He will give the provision.

So shall my word be that goeth forth out of my mouth: it shall
not return unto me void, but it shall accomplish that which I
please, and it shall prosper in the thing whereto I sent it.
Isaiah 55:11

The last bank I visited was (SB&T) Security Trust & Bank. I shared my vision with the branch manager and his response was similar to the others except he allowed me to complete a mini-application. He took a brief look at it and threw it to the side of his desk. For the very first time, I wondered did I sounded preposterous. What did the bank personnel think about me? The enemy flooded my mind with many false imaginations that I had to cast down and bring into captivity every thought to the obedience of Christ.

There were people in the Bible whose conduct seemed bizarre when they obeyed God instruction. In 2 Kings 4:1-7, is a story about a woman who was told to go around in her neighborhood and borrow as many empty vessels as she could get. I imagine she was the talk of the town. Nevertheless, she walked in faith and did what she was told without knowing what, when, or how her needs would be met. God performed a miracle in her house, and she was able to pay off all debt lived in the overflow.

God chose things the world considers foolish in order to
shame those who think they are wise. And he chose things
that are powerless to shame those who are powerful.
1 Corinthians 1:27

Approximately, a week later I received a call from the loan officer inviting me back to the bank for a very important meeting. He didn't give me any information pertaining to the meeting, only to bring my board members with me. His next words knocked me off my feet. They were "COME AFTER BUSINESS HOURS and COME TO THE BACK DOOR." You heard me right! I was not only baffled but insulted. I felt it was rude and degrading to us as African Americans / Blacks to be told those words. Although we needed his help, we were not helpless. For several days, I pondered over the meeting and was prepared to express my displeasure about the wording of the invitation.

We arrived and stood outside the back door until the loan officer opened it and invited us inside. He greeted us and told us to follow him upstairs to the second floor. After doing so we entered a large conference room where three elderly Caucasian men were seated at the end of a large table.   The man at the head introduced himself as the chairman of the bank executive board.

He asked me to restate what I shared with the loan officers during my initial visit. After doing so, he picked up my application, held it in his hand and said since you submitted this, I haven't been able to rest. I've been with this bank over 40 years and nothing has ever disturbed me more than this. I don't know why but I'm getting ready to do something that's never been done in the history of this bank. I'm approving you of a loan in the amount of $750,000 to build your church. I don't know if we will ever get our money back, but I will take full responsibility for whatever happens. You said God told you build it, if so, he will make a way.

Additionally, after construction is complete, I'm going to give you 4 months before your first payment is due. This will give you time to increase your savings.

My body was in shock, and I couldn't believe what I heard him say. I was speechless.

It felt like I had an outer body experience. Everyone was looking at me and waiting on my response. Suddenly, a flood of tears started rolling down my face and I was crying uncontrollably. The atmosphere in the room shifted and many started tearing up, including the bank executive board. After gaining my composure, I thanked them and promised to fulfill our financial obligation.

As we were leaving the room, the Holy Spirit said, "I told you it was going to be easy." Those words were resurgent and resonated in my mind repeatedly. God had given us a "BACK DOOR" and "AFTER HOURS" blessing.

What do I mean by that? I'm glad you asked. **A BACK-DOOR BLESSING** is when God orchestrates ways to bless you abnormally. Most times, we expect God to bless us a specific way or the same way He did for someone else. We tend to forget when it comes to God's Sovereignty, He is known for doing unusual and uncommon things to bless us.

For example, God did something "through the backdoor" by sending ravens to feed Elijah. Ravens were known as scavengers who ate all types of foul things.

> Then the word of the Lord came to Elijah: "Leave here,
> turn eastward, and hide in the Kerith Ravine, east of
> the Jordan. You will drink from the brook, and I have
> directed the ravens to supply you with food there."
> I Kings 17:2-4

Notice how Elijah was open-minded and strategically led by God to receive his backdoor blessing. He didn't reject his provision from God because it didn't appear or come as he had expected. He didn't complain that he was being fed by ravenous creatures. The prophet went where God instructed him, and although it was unusual and unprecedented, he received a back-door blessing.

I encourage you to be open-minded and sensitive to God's strategic plan for you. Your back-door blessing will not look like someone else's blessing, and it may not come the way you are anticipating.

An **AFTER-HOURS BLESSING occurs when the opportunity to conduct business has passed, and all doors have been closed and locked to you. Surprisingly,** God reopens spiritual doors "after hours" for only you to walk through to receive your blessing.

Many times, God intervenes "after hours" when it seems all is done, and it's too late for anything to happen. He will allow your situation to get to a point where it looks hopeless, so when He shows up and does the impossible, He only will get the glory.

In the Bible (John 11), we read the story of an impossible situation about a man named Lazarus who died after being ill. Lazarus's sisters had sent for Jesus, but instead of Jesus coming right away, he waited four days until after Lazarus's death before going to see them. The Jewish culture believed that a person was not actually accepted as being fully dead with no chance of coming back to life until after three days. Therefore, Jesus waited four days when all hope and the chances of him coming back were gone so he could demonstrate his power and get the glory. When Jesus arrived at Lazarus's tomb, he spoke the simple words, "Lazarus, come forth!" And he did! It was an "after-hours" miracle.

God desires to bless us, and He will often let us get into impossible situations so that we will witness His power, believe in Him, and recognize Him as the almighty God that He is. He also uses those seasons to prepare us for the future, to grow our faith, and to teach us patience. He delays His intervention for our good.

However, keep in mind that these periods of waiting are not just about us. Sometimes, He puts us in a desperate situation to display His glory to the people around us. In so doing, others will believe nothing is impossible for Him and that He is the Almighty God.

If you are also waiting on the Lord, don't give up! God hasn't forgotten about you, and He is not running late. In His timing, He will deliver you. He will be glorified through your trials, and when He shows up, people around you will believe in the one true and all-powerful God. You will then look back and realize it was worth the wait.

14

CHAPTER

Standing On Holy Ground

On March 27, 2004, groundbreaking services were held on the site of the future church located at 1719 Cordele Road, Albany, Georgia, with many families, friends, clergy, officials, partners, and the couple whose hearts God touched to sell us the land, Mr. and Mrs. Will Grace was in attendance.

Those appointed to participate in the groundbreaking ceremony were Ms. Forestine Lake (Church Mother), Mrs. Audra Knox (Finance Secretary), Mr. John Reid Sr. (Chairman of Deacons), Mr. Jeff Brown (General Contractor), Master Joshua Smith (8-year-old son), Elect Lady Deirdere Smith (My wife) and yours truly, Mr. Ronald Smith (Senior Pastor).

On November 14, 2004, the land was cleared, and construction was underway.

I was thrilled to finally witness the building under construction. I was there every day, walking around, praying, and talking with the workers. As soon as the foundation was laid, I called an assembly of the entire congregation, and we praised God for his mighty work.

And they sang together by course in praising and giving thanks unto the LORD; because he is good, for his mercy endureth forever toward Israel. And all the people shouted with a great shout when they praised the LORD because the foundation of the house of the LORD was laid.

Ezra 3:11

Also, I asked everyone to get a marker and write scriptures over the entire foundation so we would always be standing on the word of God.

On Sunday, July 10, 2005, we entered our new sanctuary and held our first worship service. The atmosphere was charged, and we had a glorious time. The people sang, shouted, danced, ran, and praised God with all their might. It was epic.

My first sermon was titled "This is Holy Ground." Exodus 3:5

God can't use a man until He gets him on holy ground. A holy God must have a holy man on holy ground. Holy ground is not a physical place, but a spiritual one. When God commanded Moses to take off his shoes because he was on holy ground, He was not referring to a two-by-four piece of real estate. He was talking about a spiritual state.

God called Moses from the burning bush, commanding him: The place was holy! What place? The spiritual condition he had finally come to. Moses had arrived at a place in his growth where God could get through to him. He was now at the place of reception, ready to listen. He was mature and ready to be dealt with by a holy God. Moses alone was on holy ground. So was all of Israel, even though they were at the end of their hope. I have never believed God would keep an entire nation under slavery just to give Moses time to mature into a gracious leader. Our Lord is no respecter of persons. God, in those 40 trying years, was preparing Israel as well as Moses. By way of loving judgment, the Lord was driving Israel back to holy ground - back to a hunger for Jehovah. There is what He was doing to us.

While Moses was on the mountain being stripped of all his rights - because that is what was meant by the removal of his shoes - Israel was in the valley being stripped of all human strength. Moses would have no rights; Israel, no strength. God could prove Himself strong on their behalf in no other way. The great "I AM" was being revealed!

15

CHAPTER

A Weeping Prophet

We welcomed many visitors to our new church. Shockingly, several bank board members came to a midweek bible study. I introduced them to the congregation and one gentleman asked if he could share a few words. He started by letting us know we were blessed people. He said our loan was one-of-a-kind and hasn't or will ever be done for anyone else.

As a result of its uniqueness, they were unable to follow their normal loan processing procedure. He reached inside his jacket and pulled out an appraisal. He said they came in person to share the enormous survey total of our property. His voice started to crescendo as he read our property new appraised value in the amount of $1.3 million! He said we had only used $550,000 with $750,000 in equity now available to start construction on another building. I said "Hold Up. Are you telling me we can start on another edifice and haven't made our first payment on this one yet? He looked at me with a chuckle on his face and said, "Unequivocally Yes!" God is blessing you abundantly. Once again, the Holy Spirit said, "Didn't I tell you it was going to be easy."

Everyone started rejoicing and praising God for another miracle. I told them we would contact them later with our decision.

We resolved to wait some years to build phase 2, and now we are planning phase 3. My spirit was frail, and it didn't take much for me to become emotional about what God was doing in our midst. Like the Prophet Jeremiah, you could call me a weeping prophet.

The words of Romans 8:18 never became as real to me as they were doing those days:

For I consider that the sufferings of this present time (this present life) are not worth being compared with the glory that is about to be revealed to us and in us and for us and conferred on us!

One of my favorite gospel recording artists is J.J. Hairston. He wrote a song that reverberates the words of the Apostle Paul of the scripture above titled "After This."

God specializes in things impossible;
He loves to move when all hope is lost,
Just so He can show himself strong on your behalf,
Don't give up, He'll come through for you

And there will be glory after this.
There will be victory after this.
God will turn it around,
He will bring you out.
There will be glory after this.

Whatever challenges you may be experiencing in your life, don't quit or throw in the towel; it will soon be over, and there will be glory after this.

16

CHAPTER

A Blessing In Disguise

Life's most challenging moments often serve as the channels for our greatest growth. The pain of receiving restraining orders, which forbade my return to my church as pastor, became the unforeseen blessing that propelled me to start another church.

My journey as a pastor was rooted in a deep sense of calling. From those early days at Pleasant Grove Baptist Church until today, I have discovered a profound purpose in guiding my flock through life's fluctuations. However, it all changed when I received the restraining order. The initial shock was overwhelming, a mix of disbelief, anger, and painful sorrow. This event was not just a personal setback; it felt like a derailment of my life's mission.

However, through my ordeal, I learned invaluable lessons that were transformative and enlightening catalysts for personal growth. They shaped me into a stronger, wiser, more empathetic, and resilient person.

As a pastor, my faith has always been the cornerstone of my existence. However, the restraining orders tested my faith like never before. It was during this period of brokenness that my relationship with God deepened. I leaned heavily on my faith, finding solace in prayer and scripture, which became a source of light in my darkest times. Out of the ashes emerged an opportunity to start anew.

The person I am today is a mosaic of the trials I faced. Each piece is a testament to the virtues carved from adversity. Patience became my sanctuary, empathy my guide, and strength my companion. Looking back, I see now that God was the potter, and I, the clay. Each stroke of His hand was shaping me with purpose and love. It was a divine orchestration of a masterpiece in the making, a greater future than I could have ever imagined.

To those of you facing a similar situation, remember that no trial is insurmountable with faith as your shield. Lean on your support network, listen for the whisper of hope, and keep your heart open to the lessons of adversity. Tribulations, with their capacity to transform, refine, and enlighten, are not just challenges but blessings in disguise. They are the crucibles in which our true selves are forged under the watchful eyes of a loving God. As I stand in the light of my trials, I am grateful for every wound, for they are the marks of a life richly lived and a faith deeply cherished.

When God serves restraining orders, He has a greater plan and a new place awaiting you. Always remember that God will not protect you from what He perfects you through. Life's challenges often come disguised as setbacks, but through faith and reflection, we can uncover the divine purpose behind them.

My experience of receiving restraining orders from my previous church, which prevented me from continuing as pastor, initially felt like a personal and professional crisis.

However, I soon realized that this event was a divine intervention, propelling me into new endeavors and ultimately leading to the establishment of one of the leading churches in Albany, Georgia.

When the restraining orders were first issued, the immediate impact was profound. I faced the emotional turmoil of being separated from a community I had served and loved. The loss of my pastoral role felt like a rejection of my calling and identity. However, in the midst of this crisis, I began to sense a deeper purpose behind the circumstances.

The days following the restraining orders were filled with prayer and introspection. I sought solace in my faith, asking God for understanding and direction. This period of uncertainty became a fertile ground for spiritual growth. As I distanced myself from the turmoil, I began to hear God's voice more clearly, guiding me towards new horizons.

One of the most significant blessings that emerged from this experience was the opportunity to build my own church. This new beginning allowed me to create a ministry that reflected my vision and values, free from the conflicts and constraints of the past.

Starting from scratch was both a daunting and exhilarating task. I drew upon my faith and the support of a small, dedicated group of believers. Together, we established a new church that quickly grew into one of the leading congregations in Albany, Georgia. This new church became a beacon of hope and a testament to God's provision and faithfulness.

The restraining orders also opened doors to new relationships and opportunities. Being removed from my previous church pushed me to network with other pastors, ministries, and community leaders. These connections proved invaluable in expanding my ministry and outreach.

Meeting new pastors and ministry leaders allowed me to exchange ideas and collaborate on various initiatives. These relationships enriched my ministry and broadened my perspective. I learned new approaches to leadership and community engagement, which I incorporated into my church.

God used the restraining orders to order and enlarge my steps and territory. What initially seemed like a restriction turned into an expansion of my influence and ministry. This experience taught me to trust in God's plan, even when it seemed counterintuitive.

As my new church grew, so did our impact on the community. We launched numerous outreach programs, supporting local schools, shelters, and other community organizations. This expansion was a direct result of the opportunities that arose from the initial setback. God's guidance led us to serve more people and make a more significant difference in Albany.

The journey from the initial crisis to establishing a thriving ministry was marked by significant spiritual growth and personal transformation. The challenges I faced strengthened my faith and resilience, shaping me into a more effective leader and servant of God.

Facing the unknown and stepping out in faith deepened my reliance on God. Each obstacle became an opportunity to witness

His power and provision. This period of growth solidified my trust in God's plans and His ability to turn trials into triumphs.

My experience has taught me that God's restraining orders are not punishments but divine interventions designed to guide us towards greater purposes. I want to encourage others to embrace these moments of divine redirection, trusting that God has a plan far greater than we can imagine.

To those facing similar challenges, I say: Do not resist God's restraining orders. Embrace them with faith and an open heart. These moments of redirection are opportunities for growth, new beginnings, and expanded influence. Trust in God's wisdom and timing, and you will find that your life will be transformed in ways you never thought possible.

Receiving restraining orders from my previous church was a turning point that, through faith and perseverance, became a profound blessing. This experience led to the establishment of a leading church in Albany, Georgia, the expansion of my ministry, and significant personal and spiritual growth. By embracing God's restraining orders, I discovered new opportunities and a deeper relationship with Him

In conclusion, I thank God for the restraining orders that once seemed like obstacles. They were, in fact, divine interventions that redirected my path towards greater opportunities and blessings. To anyone facing similar situations, I encourage you to embrace God's restraining hand. Trust that He is working for your good, guiding you towards His perfect plan. Let these moments be a testament to His faithfulness and a catalyst for growth in your journey. Top of Form

Printed in the United States
by Baker & Taylor Publisher Services